I0170678

STOP IT!

You're too smart to keep making Dumb Decisions

Dr. Lonnie Carton

Copyright © 2012 by Dr. Lonnie Carton

All Rights Reserved.

Cover designed by Phyllis Randall

Published by Kaye Productions

www.kayeproductions.com

ISBN 978-0-9829716-2-8

PRINTED IN THE UNITED STATES OF AMERICA

1 3 5 7 9 10 8 6 4 2

First Edition

DEDICATION

*This book is dedicated to my husband and
the smart decision I made to marry him, a
choice which blessed us both with children and
grandchldren who in the short and long term
have so positively impacted our lives.*

Table of Contents

STOP IT!

You're too smart to keep making Dumb Decisions

Preface

Every day people of all ages have decisions to make. Too often, the important ones are not well thought out. As a C.B.S. broadcast journalist heard nationwide for 3 decades, I have listened to, spoken with, and helped millions of smart people who have made dumb decisions learn to make smarter ones.

Think about Penn State University's legendary head coach, Joe Paterno. One horribly bad decision on his part in failing to adequately report or follow up on the alleged sexual molestation of young boys by one of his former coaches and not only Paterno's reputation but his life's work was destroyed. Or think of Tiger Woods whose altercations with his wife seriously blemished not only his reputation as a model athlete, but also negatively impacted his golf game. Add to these Lance Armstrong, multi medal winning bicyclist accused of using ability enhancing drugs to win his races. More additions to this list include Charlie Sheen, Lindsey Lohan, the rapper Tupac and so many other celebs and news makers whose personal and professional lives hit bottom because they made bad decisions. Closer to home some of our own local, state and national politicians have caused their families, friends, and themselves great suffering in exchange for some instant gratification. All these supposedly smart people made dumb decisions. But they are not alone, not by a long shot! Chances are, there are large numbers of not so famous people you know who get trapped in making stupid choices. Your best friend in a divorce proceeding may bad mouth her ex to their daughter, or your colleague teaching at a community college may keep pressing a coed to have a few drinks with him, or your co-worker may call in sick many times and is ultimately seen by the boss at a daytime ballgame.

Being human, it's likely even you have made some bad choices you wish you could change. While it's impossible to go back, you can move forward. The smart decision-making plan called D.A.I.S.E. shared in this book provides a new beginning for you. Plant it firmly into the soil of your strategies for making sound, sensible, successful choices and **WATCH IT GROW. GOOD LUCK.**

Chapter 1

The Party

Four people met at a party. They had not seen each other since graduating from high school ten years earlier. What was unusual about them was how much alike they were. They were all accomplished, smart, savvy young women. They had come from similar economic and ethnic backgrounds. They had all graduated college and had chosen very similar career tracks. Physically, none of the women was hands down more attractive than the other. In their brief conversation, they all professed to be doing every thing possible to "make it" personally and professionally.

The difference between them was that only Sophia was actually SATISFIED WITH HER LIFE. She alone felt "at the top of her game" socially, emotionally, and financially. Fran, Lauren and Olivia all sensed a subtle shift as Sophia talked passionately about the choices she had made since high school. She wasn't posturing like they were. Sophia honestly had become the secure, successful person that they had only imagined they would become when they parted ways at graduation.

"Okay Sophia. What's the deal? " Lauren leaped into the conversation, letting her guard down first. "How did you manage your life so well?

"Sophia smiled. "Simple," she said. "I found the **DAISE** and it changed my life."

"Very funny" Lauren said, "Never knew you to be the crunchy granola type in high school unless this is your newest makeover secret and you're holding back on us."

Actually, Sophia was not joking or being secretive; she was telling the truth. Her entire life had been changed by **DAISE** and SO CAN YOURS!

Whether you are a young professional, single or married, a parent or a grandparent, male or female, **DAISE** can help you make better decisions.

The **DAISE** Sophia found is not the garden variety DAISY. That daisy is a simple flower. Often it is used in game fashion to figure out whether or not someone loves you or whether you should make one choice or the other. As each petal is pulled off, the petal puller recites, "He loves me, he loves me not" or "I'll do it, I won't do it." The final decision is pure chance. It depends on the number of petals the flower has, and on whether or not the petal puller begins with being loved, not being loved, doing something, or not doing it. The **DAISE** on the other hand, is not a game of chance. It is a sure, simple way for all those who learn the rules to put themselves in control of their decisions and their life choices.

Finding smart solutions to the everyday challenges and problems facing you is much too important to leave to chance. Your self worth, security, satisfaction, and success depend on how skillful you are in making smart rather than stupid choices.

Think about it! Seven days a week, three hundred and sixty five days a year, from the time you awaken each morning to the time you go to bed, you are making choices: what clothes to wear, whether to get your energy boost from a healthy breakfast or from the overpriced java jolt you pick up on your way to work, what to say to a colleague who continually palms off on you the work she's supposed to do, whether to renew your magazine subscriptions, know how to treat a friend who has been gossiping behind your back, or whether to continue giving your charitable donations.

Many of the choices are simple and automatic. Others are complicated and take more time to figure out. What to do about a "significant other" who just won't commit; how to deal with a spouse who's unfaithful or a bully; what action to take with a child or grandchild who is disrespectful and unappreciative; how to keep peace with the in-laws; what to do about job burn-out; and where to get help in coming to grips with feeling totally stressed out or depressed are some of the more challenging problems.

No matter how clumsy or clueless you have been in making good choices up to now, you can make better ones. Like that garden-variety daisy which opens when the day starts and symbolizes new beginnings, **DAISE** is Your new beginning. So pick this **DAISE** and start learning the strategies for smart decisions.

Listed below are five of the ways most people decide what to say, do, or in some cases even think. Do any of them describe how you make decisions?

1. I let what I imagine other people will think of me make my choices for me.

2. I make hasty and often unwise decisions without fully looking at all my options.

3. I delay making decisions because I'm afraid I'll make the wrong ones.

4. I often make the same mistakes over again because I'm uncomfortable thinking "outside the box" or trying a different way to solve problems.

5. I confidently and calmly make most choices based on clearly thinking about:

   a. All the alternatives I have.

   b. What the one I choose will gain or lose for me and others in the short and long term.

Be honest now! Do you sometimes or often use the first four ways to make decisions? Can you guess what choice making method Sophia uses? What about her three high school friends?

You're right! For Lauren who leaps first, it's the quick pick she's addicted to. She fails to take the time to add up the many options or alternatives she actually has. She's an early mover and while sometimes that head start keeps her ahead of the crowd, it can also trip her up. For Olivia it's the fear of trying anything new that guides her decision making. Call her Olivia Oldshoes, because just like she clings to her favorite worn and ratty bedroom slippers, she chooses to stick with the kind of choices she has made in the past. It just feels good, and it's comfortable, and it's safe. It also makes it almost impossible for her to move beyond her comfort zone to take a chance on any opportunity for a different or better outcome.

As for Fran, she's the foot dragger. She never catches the golden ring of physical, social, emotional or economic happiness because she waits too long. Usually by waiting so long, the moment of choice completely passes her by and the decision is taken out of her hands.

If you have been lucky enough to avoid using the dumb decision-making strategies that have locked in Lauren, Olivia and Fran, what method do you use? Have the decisions you've made in the past proven to be the right ones? **NO? NOT AS OFTEN AS YOU'D LIKE?**

Not to worry...help is on the way.

Chapter 2

Here's D.A.I.S.E.

DEFINE/DECIDE what decision you have to make or problem you want to solve.

ADD up all the choices you have in making / solving it.

INVESTIGATE how smart or stupid each choice or solution would be.

SELECT the one you think best and try it.

EVALUATE the choice you made. Did it solve or at least reduce your problem? How? Why not?

What keeps many of us from making the right decision the first time around is that once we make it we don't take the time to evaluate whether that decision is the best one we could have made. Whether we're pressed for time, too stressed out, or just want out of the decision-making process, we just go for it.

One of the real beauties of **DAISE** is that the **"I"** step protects you against making this mistake.

If you find the choice you made isn't working as well as you'd like, you can go back and take a look at other alternatives you've already had a chance to INVESTIGATE. Be sure to use the **EVALUATE** step as a guide to making a better decision next time around.

Learning why a choice didn't work (**EVALUATING**) can be almost as important as **SELECTING** the right one the first time around.

As the ancient Chinese philosopher warned:

"He who makes one mistake and does not learn from it makes two mistakes."

Chapter 3

Using D.A.I.S.E.

Now that you're familiar with what good decision making requires, how can you use **DAISE** to be successful at it?

Getting the know-how that empowered Sophia to change her life relies on three basic truths. Smart people who make dumb decisions do not take these truths into account when they make their decisions.

1. Every decision has both short and long term consequences.

2. Every decision affects not only the decision maker but also other people.

3. Every decision affects people in different ways (socially, physically, emotionally, economically and morally).

Bad decision makers not only pay no attention to these three truths, they also fail to realize that practice does not always make perfect. People who practice the wrong thing in the wrong way over and over again never become successful. Lauren, Olivia and Fran are proof of this.

Begin your own success story by gaining practice in filling out the chart on the next page. Think back to a time you had to make an important choice. Perhaps you decided to break up with a long time significant other. Maybe you thought about quitting a job you didn't like and going back to school. Or imagine that you, yourself are one of the hundreds of thousands of people of all ages underemployed or with no job at all. Should you move back in with your parents until the economy improves?

For many people today the impact of being jobless is forcing them to make tough decisions. More and more of them have to decide whether or not to move back in with their parents. Maybe some of your unemployed or underemployed friends or you, yourself, are faced with having to make this difficult decision.

Use the chart below to measure how moving back home might affect YOU.

	Today	In The Future
Health		
Emotions		
Social Life		
Pocketbook		
Values		

In each of the five categories put a **+** (plus) if you believe the decision to "move back" would have a positive impact on your life. Put a **–** (minus) if you think there would be negative consequences. Leave the box blank if you think there would be no impact.

Since making a smart choice requires thinking of both the short and long term consequences of your action, enter the effect in both the **TODAY** and **IN THE FUTURE** columns.

Since **DAISE** is new to you, try using the following questions as a guide for the **INVESTIGATE** step. They could give you the information needed to make a more clever choice.

- Would you feel like a failure because you had to move back home?

- Would you be upset about having to spend the little money you still have saved to pay your parents for room and board.

- Now that you will live as an adult in your parent's home will you be treated like one?

- Will you feel resentful if you're expected to drive your parents to doctor appointments, shopping, visiting friends?

- Will you be comfortable having no privacy when your friends come over?

- Will you be able to handle it when parents, relatives and neighbors make suggestions about what you should be doing to get a job?

There are no right or wrong answers. All human beings are different. It's perfectly natural for two people reading the same book or watching the same T.V. program to have different takes on what they see and hear.

Why? Because what a person gets out of a book, movie, TV show or even a conversation depends upon the attitudes and experiences he or she brings to it.

So just give it your best guess as to how your health, emotions, social life, pocketbook and values would be negatively or positively impacted if you chose to move back home.

Once you are finished, turn the page to see how some other people filled in the boxes and why.

	Today	In The Future
Health	+	+
Emotions	−	
Social Life	+	−
Pocketbook	+	+
Values	+	

The following pages describe the results of their **INVESTIGATIONS**.

TODAY
(SHORT TERM)

HEALTH

Assuming that your parents serve healthy meals rather than the fast food, on-the-run snacks or cheaper groceries you've been buying and eating, there is likely to be an improvement in your health. There would be an additional positive impact if you used your free time to regularly workout.

Health	+

EMOTIONS

Your sense of failure and loss of independence could cause you to suffer the kind of shame and fear which would have a negative impact. The resulting anxiety could lead to depression.

Emotions	−

SOCIAL LIFE

You have more free time to meet with your old friends and make new friends by involving yourself in community activities and discovering new interests.

Social Life	+

POCKETBOOK

Unless the rent you have to pay living at home is more than what it would cost living in your own apartment and buying your own food, your pocketbook would be impacted.

Pocketbook	+

VALUES

Although they may not admit it, many parents, especially those who live alone, would enjoy another person in the home not only for companionship but for the safety and security it brings. If family loyalty, responsibility, and unselfishness are some of the principles by which you fashion your life, chances are you'd have a "feeling good " result.

Values	+

IN THE FUTURE

(LONG TERM)

Neither a crystal ball nor a giant magnifying glass can exactly predict what the future holds. However using your past experience and best judgement, you should be able to make a pretty good guess.

HEALTH

The introduction to healthy food and its benefits could help make a positive change in your own buying and eating habits when you move out and get a job. Also, the routine you began in your patent's home of spending time walking, exercising and paying attention to your physical well being might continue as a healthy habit.

Health	+

EMOTIONS

It could take a long time to find a well paying, secure enough job to enable you to move out. The long-term emotional impact of being back at home could have negative or positive consequences. This would depend largely on the relationship between you and your parents, your patience and theirs, and your emotional stability and level of confidence in yourself.

You would be negatively impacted if you realized you were becoming a burden on your parents and even more fearful because there were no job prospects yet in sight. You could be positively impacted if you still felt safer and more secure knowing where your next meal was coming from and that no matter how much longer it took to get a job, you could be assured of your parent's continued support. Leave this box blank.

Emotions	

SOCIAL LIFE

It is likely that in the future, the positive social impact experienced in the short term (Today) would turn into a negative. Even good friends may begin to resent the fact that you have so much free time. They may be pissed off that you continue to receive unemployment benefits without seeming to make much of an effort to find a paying job while they have to get up and go to work each day.

Social Life	–

POCKETBOOK

Even if you were charged a nominal fee for room and board, the amount is likely to be much less than having to support yourself renting and eating on your own. You would also be able to keep more of the money you had saved before moving in with your folks as well as any extra money from your unemployment check or part time work you might get.

Pocketbook	+

VALUES

Health, wealth, social life and emotions can change. Values are more stable. If it is important for you to give back to others, like your family, as well as take from them, your values will be positively supported. If however, what you value most is your own self interest, privacy and desire for independence, the impact would be negative. Leave this box blank.

Values	

After **INVESTIGATING** the consequences of any decision you have to make, chances are even the one you actually **SELECTED** will not score all positives. A way to check if your selection was the best one is to count how many positive impacts it offered in the short and long term.

Evaluate the decision:

If you score more positive impacts than negative ones in the areas most important to you, (health, emotions, social life, pocketbook and values) you've probably made a smart choice. **AT LEAST FOR YOU !!**

But what about the other people affected by what you do?

Making smart decisions, like life itself, requires balancing what you have to give for what you get. In the next chapter you will become more skillful in acquiring this balance as you learn about Robert's EXPENSIVE MISTAKE.

Chapter 4

The Expensive Mistake

Robert had been shopping for some time for a birthday gift for his wife. Because his work hours had been cut, he was not able to spend as much on the gift as he had wanted. On his lunch break he went into a nearby boutique and found a cashmere sweater that had been reduced. When he went to pay for it there was a line of customers ahead of him and a small sign on the counter that read, "Sorry for any delay. I'm new on the job."

Back in his office, Robert checked the present to insert a card. To his surprise he saw there was a small box with a diamond tennis bracelet in the bag along with the sweater. Robert was stunned. Then he remembered seeing the bracelet among the purchases on the counter from the customer in front of him. What had probably happened is that the new cashier, in her lack of experience and her rush to keep up with the customers, had mistakenly swept the small box into his bag. What should Robert do?

Do **D.A.I.S.E.**

DEFINE THE PROBLEM:

WHAT SHOULD ROBERT DO WITH THE DIAMOND BRACELET?

ADD UP THE CHOICES:

1. *Give his wife both gifts.*

2. *Return the diamond bracelet to the boutique.*

3 *Take the jewelry back for a cash refund claiming his wife had gotten it as a gift from her Mom and didn't have a receipt.*

4 *Give his wife the diamond bracelet for her next birthday.*

5. *Take it to a pawn shop.*

INVESTIGATE THE CHOICES:

#1 TOO MUCH TOO SOON

In the short term, Robert would have looked like a wonderful husband by giving his wife two expensive gifts for one birthday. In the long term, having set such a high level of expectation in gift giving, he would have had a lot of difficulty measuring up to that the next time around. The two gifts could also raise questions with his wife. Knowing that her husband's hours at work had been cut, she might ask why he spent so much money at this time or even insist he return one of the gifts. If she insists the more expensive one be returned what does Robert do then?

#2: DO THE RIGHT THING

A rose by any other name would smell as sweet. Dishonesty, even if it is the result of an accident, is still dishonesty.

As soon as Robert realized he had not paid for the diamond bracelet and decided not to return it, it could be considered stolen property. Could he live with that knowledge morally? Would his conscience let him? Isn't it likely that he would get a guilt feeling each time his wife wore the jewelry or whenever any friends remarked what a wonderful husband he was to give her such an extraordinary gift ?

If this reminder from his conscience didn't bother Robert, what about his concern for the innocent woman who had actually paid for the bracelet? Even with the receipt there was no guarantee she would get her money back. After all, there was no way for her to prove she didn't have the tennis bracelet in her bag when she left the store. Robert would also have avoided causing the manager frustration and uncertainty about what to do. Also, if Robert had returned the jewelry promptly, his wife would have been protected from having suspicions of the dishonesty of a man whom she trusted. This loss of trust could cause her to be suspicious about other things he told her. Most importantly, he would have the chance to feel good about doing the right thing.

#3: POINT OF NO RETURN

Take the bracelet to the boutique. Advise the manager that you want to return it for a cash refund but you do not have the receipt nor know what it cost. That is because it was a gift to your wife from her mother.

It is said money is the root of all evil. The fact that Robert was now earning less at his job might encourage him to do double duty dishonesty. In the short term, he could make excuses for his decision in this way. He already had the bracelet in his possession. No one knew he had it. He didn't actually steal it.

And, most important, he could really use the money.

In the long term, yes, he would be getting money but at what cost? What if the woman who actually paid for the bracelet had already informed the store that it was not in her bag? How could Robert prove he had accidentally received the jewelry and not stolen it in order to resell it?

Robert wasn't thinking clearly enough about not being the only player in the choices he made.

But he did give some thought to what would probably happen if he tried to cash in.

He figured that he wouldn't be causing the woman who had actually purchased the bracelet any real harm, especially if she were a good customer. The manager would see her receipt and probably acknowledge that with the new cashier a mistake had been made.

Either way, Robert assured himself, the store was insured and only the insurance company would take the hit.

#4: A PENNY SAVED IS A PENNY EARNED

What a deal! Save not only money which he really didn't have much of and save time not having to search around for a birthday gift next year.

But who would be saving Robert's sense of self and pride as an honorable man?

In the children's book Pinocchio, Pinocchio's partner Jiminy Cricket serves as the wooden headed boy's conscience. He helps him learn right from wrong. Human beings do not come with Jiminy Crickets on their shoulders but they do come with brains and a conscience. No matter how many ways it is looked at or how long it takes, keeping what doesn't belong to you is no better than stealing it in the first place.

#5: *TELL IT TO THE JUDGE*

Pawn shops are regularly checked by the police department and security cameras are on twenty-four seven. If the diamond bracelet is worth a substantial amount, the money Robert might get for it probably wouldn't cover his bail to get out of jail until his trial. Even more critical, it would not be easy for him to make a jury believe he didn't steal the bracelet in the first place. He had no receipt for the purchase, nor any evidence to prove it was a gift to his wife.

His story about accidentally finding it in his bag would prove hard to believe. This would become even more damaging because he failed to return the item to the boutique right away.

Roberts dumb decision is a perfect example of how a small, accidental situation, can grow into a mountain of trouble. He took the quick fix, short-term gain never thinking ahead to the long term pain that could result.

He did not immediately return the diamond bracelet to the boutique. Nor did he give his wife both the sweater and the bracelet for her birthday. Instead, he kept the "hot" piece of jewelry locked in the desk in his office,

A few days of clear thinking led him to the conclusion that he could not risk a pawn shop. And while the money he could get from the boutique by retuning the bracelet as an item that had been gifted to his wife by her mother seemed almost too tempting to give up, he decided not to. He doubted he had the courage to pull off that dishonest scheme. Besides, even if it worked, what he needed now was cold cash not a credit receipt to purchase something else in the store.

"Maybe it would be worth taking the chance if the store sold food, gas or mortgage payments," he laughed to himself.

After another week of soul searching, fear and confusion, Robert found himself in the position of Frannie Footdragger. Remember her? She was one of the four female friends introduced in the first few pages of this book. She too waited too long before making up her mind.

As is too often true of anyone who waits too long to make a decision, the choice is often taken out of his or her hands. New situations arise which limit or change the individual's decision making opportunity.

In Robert's case, all the time he took planning and thinking what he could get away with, limited him from doing the honest thing which was to promptly return the bracelet. To attempt to return it now would very likely raise suspicions about why he took so long for its return. For an item of such an expensive nature, the store would surely have been notified by the buyer on the first day. This would indicate to the store that it had been in Robert's possession for a long time.

Now the young husband was left with only one choice. A dishonest one! Keep the bracelet for a year and then give it to his wife for her birthday.

This is what Robert finally did. But he is fearfully hoping that the economic situation of his company will improve enough to put him back to work as a full time employee. If that does not happen, he does not know what he will tell his wife when he gives her the bracelet. Will she insist he return it for the money they need to live on? Then what?

Making a bad decision is like falling into quicksand. The more you try to get out of it, the deeper you are sucked in.

Test the results of a bad decision on the simple D.A.I.S.E. chart below: In the five categories listed, put a plus or a minus in the boxes which rate whether Robert's decision would have a negative or a positive effect. Remember, there is no right or wrong answer. Just use your best judgment and experience.

	Today	In The Future
Health		
Emotions		
Social Life		
Pocketbook		
Values		

Now, turn the page for a more detailed review of the **INVESTIGATION** steps in Robert's decision making.

TODAY

HEALTH

If you've ever been in a situation where you had to choose between telling the truth or being dishonest, you know that the choice you make impacts your health. In most cases, telling the truth makes you feel better. There's an immediate relief in no longer having to worry about what may happen when your lies are revealed. The positive impact can be compared to the removal of a heavy weight being carried around on your shoulders night and day.

Your concentration level, your ability to get a good night's sleep, and the general feeling of satisfaction you gain by having done the right thing also improves your well being.

Robert's dishonesty makes it impossible for him to enjoy any of these benefits. Put a minus in the Health box.

Health	–

EMOTIONS

Like Siamese twins, the connection between the human body and mind is very strong. The physical stress of being trapped by making a bad decision often results in limitless anxiety. Feelings of shame, guilt and fear are also common. Robert's dishonesty is a good example of a bad decision. Put a minus in the Emotions box.

Emotions	−

SOCIAL LIFE

Telling the truth can either strengthen or strangle social life. Much depends on what is said, how it is said, including body language, and when. Other factors such as whether you were asked for the information, were forced to give it, or gave it voluntarily also determine its negative or positive impact. In Robert's case, since no one knew of his dishonesty, there would probably be no effect on his social life.

Social Life	

POCKETBOOK

Several of the choices Robert considered seriously and nearly selected are good examples of the adage; Oh what a tangled web we weave when first we practice to deceive. Had he tried returning the bracelet to the boutique or bringing it to a pawn shop, there might have been a positive impact on his pocketbook. But his indecision, bad judgment and fear prevented that. In the short term, Robert's choice had no impact on his pocketbook. Leave the box blank.

Pocketbook	

VALUES

What we know about Robert is that he values money more than honesty. Since there is little chance his decision will result in gaining more of the cash he wants, put a minus in the box

Values	−

IN THE FUTURE

HEALTH

Over time, the strain of trying to avoid getting caught increases the kind of pressure which can trigger health problems. Some of these are a rise in blood pressure, fatigue, cholesterol levels, and excess weight. Put a minus for negative impact on health.

Health	−

EMOTIONS

Constant worrying makes people emotional basket cases. Even if Robert keeps the tennis bracelet well hidden for the many months before he can give it to his wife for her birthday, he is likely to be constantly worrying. What will he say if his wife's curiosity is aroused? What will he tell her if she questions how he could afford such an expensive item? What if she asks or checks their credit card bills to see what it cost? What if Robert loses his job and his wife insists he get the money back for the jewelry? Robert's worry is real. Put a negative in the box under emotions.

Emotions	–

SOCIAL LIFE

If in the presence of his wife, relatives and friends he can keep smiling on the outside while crying on the inside, no one may ever learn of Robert's lack of honesty. Consequently, his social life is not likely to be impacted by his unwise choice. Leave social life blank.

Social Life	

POCKETBOOK

By giving the "stolen item" as a birthday gift, Robert does save the money he would have had to spend to buy his wife her present.

Pocketbook	+

VALUES

Hopefully the painful negative impacts of health, emotion and values experienced by Robert in the TODAY boxes and in his health and emotions IN THE FUTURE boxes will show him the value of HONESTY over greed. In this way his principles and code of ethical behavior would be positively impacted. Put a plus in the Values box.

Values	+

Chart how will others be affected

Robert's chart clearly shows that in both the short and long term his decision had negative consequences for him. Check the **INVESTIGATION** below to see how other people were affected by his choice.

OTHERS - TODAY

HEALTH

The needless aggravation, time and energy spent by the woman who paid for the bracelet will undoubtedly have a negative impact upon her well being. The boutique manager's stress level is also likely to be heightened if he is not quickly able to satisfy the customer's request for a new bracelet or refund.

It is possible that any extended argument that may ensue between them would not only negatively affect their patience and fatigue level but could result in a physical altercation. Put a minus in the health box.

Health	–

EMOTIONS

The frustration, anger and even desperation felt by a person who is telling the truth but not believed creates a high level of emotional distress. Many characterize it as feeling you are beating your head against a stone wall.

42

Since it is highly unlikely that the manager will immediately take the woman's word that the expensive jewelry was not in her package, both she and the combatant manager are bound to be negatively impacted by Robert's dishonesty. Mark a minus in the emotion's box.

Emotions	–

SOCIAL LIFE

If or until Robert's untruthfulness to his wife is discovered there is likely to be no impact on her social life.

Social Life	

POCKETBOOK

The boutique manager may not believe the woman's story about the missing bracelet. He may inform her that it was her responsibility to check to make sure she had the expensive bracelet in her bag after she paid for it. He may challenge her by questioning whether it could have fallen out of her bag outside the store. If so, her carelessness would certainly not be the boutique's responsibility. This would bolster the manager's claim that it is simply not the store's policy to replace or give a refund in a case with so little evidence except a receipt for the purchase.

These decisions would result in the customer not only losing her bracelet, but the money she spent on it in the first place.

If the boutique agreed to replace the tennis bracelet or refund its value, the store or its insurance company would have to take the economic hit. Put a minus in the Pocketbook box.

Pocketbook	−

VALUES

If Robert's wife ever found out about her husband's dishonesty, the trust she had in him could be negatively shaken. Similarly the values of the actual buyer of the jewelry could be negatively impacted when—despite the fact that she told the truth—the honesty, cooperation and justice she expected did not materialize.

Values	–

SELECT THE BEST CHOICE:

The three integral parts of smart decision making are:

1. How your decision affects you Today and in the Future.

2. How your decision affects Others.

2. How your decision impacts the most important parts of your life and those of others.

Look back now on the boxes filled out in the table scoring Roberts decision to be keep the bracelet.

In the TODAY column he scores three negative impacts out of five with three blanks. In the IN THE FUTURE column he scores two negatives, two positives and one blank. Combining both the short and long term impact for himself and others, Robert's score is a weak two positives.

This is the **DAISE** chart **investigating** Robert's choice and how it would affect him:

	Today	In The Future
Health	−	−
Emotions	−	−
Social Life		
Pocketbook	−	+
Values		+

While this chart indicates how it would affect others"

	Today	In The Future
Health	−	−
Emotions	−	−
Social Life		
Pocketbook	−	
Values	−	−

If Robert had used **DAISE** charts to **INVESTIGATE** his choices, he probably would have **SELECTED** a different one.

Evaluate the decision:

If you were being reviewed in the company for which you work, two positives out of twenty might have you ending up in the jobless ranks. Good decisions too, are characterized by positive results.

Not only the number of positive impacts but also the kind of positive impacts are important. These things are highly individual. Different decision makers have different areas of concern. Some might choose the importance of POCKETBOOK over SOCIAL LIFE. Others may strive to get a positive impact in HEALTH or EMOTIONS.

Another factor which enters into the scoring is the decision maker's code of ethics. Some personal values may contribute to the health and happiness of those living by them; the same actions or attitudes may have a negative effect for those on whom they are imposed. For example, bullies of all ages value power and control. They do not care about the physical, verbal, social or emotional abuse their actions cause the victims. Gang members value loyalty to the gang at all costs. Many would choose going to jail rather than "snitching" on some other member Unlike the criminal and conscienceless members of society, most decent people value compassion, cooperation, trust, honesty and justice.

We can not know for sure what Robert's values are. But we can make a good guess that honesty is not one of them.

In all the familiar smart and stupid decisions which will be presented in the next few chapters remember this important goal of **DAISE.** Smart decisions create as many positive results as possible both for the decision maker and for those whose lives are affected by that decision.

Chapter 5

I Can't Lose Weight

You seem to be a fast learner! But just to make sure, try your **DAISE** skills on one of the weightiest problems millions of men, women and even children have to deal with every day...unwanted fat.

This is Ellen's situation. Maybe it's the same one that's bugging someone you know or even you.

It's not that she hasn't tried getting rid of the excess baggage she's been carrying around on her. She has! But with little success.

Ellen has swallowed diet pills, tried two or three different weight loss programs, followed the many no sugar, low carb, limited calories taste torturing suggestions found on the Internet.

She's ridden her bike the three miles and back to the supermarket, jogged almost to China on the treadmill and climbed rather than taken the elevator up to her third floor workplace.

But the numbers on her scale don't move.

The only body loss that ever resulted was in sweat not pounds. If Ellen or any of her overweight or obese friends asked for your advice, what would you tell them to do?

Do D.A.I.S.E.

DEFINE THE PROBLEM:

WHAT CAN BE DONE TO LOSE ALL THE UNWANTED POUNDS?

ADD UP ALL THE CHOICES:

1. *Take smaller portions.*

2. *Eat, drink and be miserable.*

3. *Stop eating out.*

4. *Get a medical check up.*

5. *Shop smarter.*

6. *Find a partner.*

7. See a "shrink".

8. Consider Weight Loss Surgery.

INVESTIGATE THE CHOICES:

#1: TAKE SMALLER PORTIONS

Not only what you eat but how much you eat contributes to weight loss or gain. Try using smaller plates. Really! And never take second helpings.

If you use a regular sized plate, once you've put on what you plan to eat for that meal, take half of it away and save it for tomorrow's meal or freeze it for later.

While cutting down on the daily intake, eat smarter. If Ellen chose to go on a daily diet of twenty cups of fresh vegetables and fruit rather than just five cups of potato chips, ice cream or chocolate candy, her chances of losing weight are much better with the 20 cups of healthy food than the 5 cups of junk food.

In the short term, less is more. Eating less, and especially less sugar filled, high carb, high caloric food, is more healthy and weight reducing than pigging out.

In the long term smaller portions and the elimination of most of the fat factory foods is a slow process.

For those who have ten or less pounds to lose it could be a good choice if they can muster their will power and control themselves. Ellen, who appears to be in much worse shape, may need to find a different way to take off the pounds.

#2: EAT, DRINK, AND BE MISERABLE

In the short term, eating, and drinking all you want, anytime you want sounds like a dream come true. Actually, it's a long term nightmare.

All those extra ounces and pounds Ellen is carrying increase her chances of developing heart disease, diabetes, high blood pressure, hypertension, and high cholesterol. Dangerous as the physical risks are, there are usually painful social and emotional consequences.

In both the short and long term, large numbers of adults and even teenagers who would never judge a book by its cover, unfairly and cruelly judge the overweight and obese. Fat people are scorned as weak and lacking self control. They are ridiculed for pigging out so much that they have become as unattractive as the animals for whom their physical appearances is named.

In a society which worships looks and lifestyle.... THIN IS IN and STOUT IS OUT. This negative attitude regarding size makes it difficult for those who carry excess weight to feel good about themselves emotionally. It also makes it more difficult socially to find and keep friends.

Eating, drinking and being miserable doesn't seem like a good decision for Ellen. Help her find a better way to eat, drink and be MERRILY happy and healthy.

#3: STOP EATING OUT OR BRINGING IN FAST FOOD (which is often loaded with fat, high calories and carbs)

Anyone who has been there, done that, understands how difficult it is to choose one or two tempting appetizers, entrees, or desserts from a large restaurant menu.

For those who haven't had this experience, try this joke on for size.

A waitress went over to the table of a customer who seemed to be having trouble giving his order. He had been studying the menu for over ten minutes.

"Are you ready to order now?" she asked.

The customer replied, "I just can't seem to choose. Everything looks so good."

Finally, after a few minutes more he said, "Why don't you just bring me one of each?"

Those who eat out often find themselves unable to decide what they want. As a result, they order too much. That's why restaurants supply so many doggie bags and care packages for the take home leftovers.

In the short and long term, home cooking is a good way to control both the amount of food eaten and the kind. Not only is it likely that eating in will result in losing pounds, but also in saving money.

#4: GET A MEDICAL CHECK UP

There's more to being fat than eating too much of the wrong food or exercising too little. The body's endocrine system is often to blame.

The thyroid, a gland in the endocrine system, secretes hormones directly into the blood and lymph system. These hormones (body chemicals) control appetite, metabolism and growth. Simply stated, if the thyroid is not working properly, it is not able to burn off the fat taken in the form of food.

Look at it this way. If Ellen's car suddenly started to eat up much more gas than usual and got far fewer miles per gallon what choices would she have to fix the problem? She could try buying higher octane gas or drive at a lower speed. She could ask a friend's advice or even take out all the junk she keeps in her trunk in the hope of making her car less heavy for the engine to pull.

She might even decide to trade in for a smaller car.

Or she could make the smarter and less time consuming decision to take her auto to a trusted car mechanic.

It makes much more sense to find out why something is happening before deciding what to do about it. A medical doctor would understand the working of Ellen's thyroid, and endocrine system and all other aspects of her physical health in the same way a mechanic would be able to diagnosis what's wrong with her car.

In putting first things first, Ellen would be making a smart, safe first choice by getting a complete medical check up. This should also include getting from the doctor the nutritional guidance to begin her battle to lose weight and keep it off.

#5: SHOP SMARTER

DO NOT PASS GOing to the grocery store without a shopping list.

Just like Santa is "making a list and checking it twice," put on your list only those foods you need that week that are "nice" and healthy.

Making a shopping list filled with all kinds and colors of fresh vegetables and fruits would probably give Ellen a good head start in changing her eating habits.

It would also help to:

  a. *Only buy items from the list.*
  b. *Avoid using coupons for food she would never normally buy.*
  c. *Fight the urge to slip into her basket all the eye catching and taste tempting snacks advertised on television and in the store circulars.*

#6: FIND A PARTNER

Not only are two heads better than one, so are two bodies.

Get a companion to walk, bike, take a diet workshop with, or even share checking out web sites for the most reliable information on not only the physical and social ramifications of being overweight but also the emotional and economic ones. This togetherness is likely to not only double the pleasure, but double each partner's commitment to stay on whatever weight loss decision is chosen.

Once the partners set realistic goals for working together, their individual sense of pride and competitive spirit should give them twice as much motivation as trying to lose weight on their own. If Ellen can find someone with whom to join forces she would probably increase her will power to shop smarter, eat healthier and exercise more.

#7: SEE A "SHRINK"

Getting fat and staying fat may be not only a physical problem but an emotional one. The mind body connection is very strong. If there is a deep seated reason why Ellen can't or won't live a healthier, happier lifestyle, that problem needs to be addressed at the same time or even before the weight loss effort can succeed.

#8: CONSIDER WEIGHT LOSS SURGERY

Laparoscopic surgery is only for people who are 100 pounds or more above their ideal body weight. This is measured by standardized weight height tables.

There is long and careful preparation by medical specialists before this surgery can be performed. It includes not only physical tests but psychological analysis to determine the persons suitability for this type of operation. It would usually be a last resort for severely obese people who have tried and failed with other weight reduction programs.

Obesity affects three to five percent of the US adult population and growing numbers of children. It is life threatening in terms of hypertension, coronary artery disease and diabetes to name a few. For this reason it is a viable choice only for all those who fit in the severely overweight category.

SELECT THE BEST CHOICE:

When there are many options from which to choose, selecting more than one, either together or one soon after the other, may be a smart decision.

In Ellen's situation, number 4, getting a medical checkup, should undoubtedly be her first selection.

At the same time, by adding choices one, five and six, she has nothing to lose but the flab, fatigue and frustration that her excess baggage has created.

EVALUATE THE DECISION:

There is no safe, successful quick-fix or magic pill for losing large amounts of weight. Think of it this way. How long did it take Ellen to put on that weight? How many months or years has it been since she fit into a size 10, 12 or 14 dress?

In understanding the difference between making smart decisions about her weight loss and dumb ones, Ellen can look forward to having the patience, conviction, and motivation to be happier and healthier in both body and mind.

Chapter 6

Should I Quit

It always seems easier to solve other people's problems than our own. If you were a talk show host interviewing a young woman who needed help making the right decision, how would you advise her?

Here's what she says:

> My employer is getting on my nerves big time. He is always telling me what to do, both on the job and even in my personal life. I have been working for him for over two years but I still feel he is micromanaging me. He often gives me unwanted and unasked for advice. He asks for my professional opinion and then doesn't give me a chance to present my views and suggestions. It's getting me so frustrated that I'm beginning to feel insecure about making the right decisions for myself personally and professionally.

What guidance would you give her using **DAISE** as your guide?

DEFINE the problem that needs to be solved. Keeping a sharp focus on the most important thing to resolve here the problem is:

What can be done about a boss who gets involved in your work to the point of getting in the way?

ADD up all your choices (alternatives) in making this decision. This process is called brainstorming and it is a learned skill. It requires opening your mind to any and all options without judging them. Neither Lauren, who leapt forward with hasty decisions, nor Olivia, who was reluctant to take risks and preferred to make safe choices, used brainstorming in their decision making process.

Here are some of the options or choices you have. You may think of others. Which ones do you believe would work?

1. *Grin and bear it*

    Don't disrupt the status quo. It works for the boss. You have your job. Suck it up and keep your head down. This choice is one Fran the Foot dragger might have kicked around for a while. Saying nothing is a choice!

2. *Tell him where to get off clearly and firmly*

    Let your boss know that you don't need advice nor do you want it. You're perfectly capable of deciding for yourself what to do professionally and personally. This is the "bull in the china shop" approach that Lauren probably used quite often.

3. *Talk to your boss calmly and courteously*

    Explain what is bothering you. Take a deep breath and find the courage and an appropriate time to bring the issue to his attention.

4. *Send him a message by example*

    Look for ways and times to give your boss "unasked for advice." Could he have run that last meeting better? Tell him. Could he have handled his client more professionally during the video conference? Tell him. This choice is used in the hopes that the offender (your boss) will get the message, feel how upsetting it is to be given unwanted advice, and stop bugging you.

Here are a few more possibilities.

5. *Go to the top*

Make your complaints to your boss's boss or the owner of the company. Report what has been happening and ask for help. With this you are reaching out to and relying on a different power base to solve your problem.

6. *Quit your job*

This is the "haste makes waste" approach that some people would choose even in a difficult economy. It's an action that could create more problems than it solves. But it is an option.

OTHER CHOICES?

Now that you have **DEFINED** the problem in a clear and concise way and **ADDED** up and identified a number of choices and options through brainstorming it is time to **INVESTIGATE** your choices.

INVESTIGATE THE CHOICES:

Think about the risk associated with each of the options. What good or bad consequences might result from making a decision based on each of them?

Remind the unhappy worker to look at short term and long term impact of the consequences. How will she be affected? How will others be affected?

Since you are still learning to use **DAISE** we'll help by doing the **INVESTIGATING** for you.

#1: GRIN AND BEAR IT

Any time a problem or situation makes you feel uncomfortable, angry, guilty, or fearful, you cannot drag your feet. Do something about it. Getting your frustrations and feelings out in the open is much smarter than keeping them bottled up inside. It's a lot healthier too. Here's why:

Think of yourself as a Pyrex teapot with water boiling inside. The open spout of the teapot serves as a vent for letting out the steam. Tightly close that vent while continuing to boil the water and sooner or later what happens? The pressure of the steam that is unable to get out causes the pot to crack and even EXPLODE.

Human emotions are like a tightly closed teapot with water boiling inside. When the pressure gets too hot to handle, and the steam of fury or frustration has no way to escape. YOU crack and explode.

Repressing feelings rather than expressing them damages you not only emotionally but also physically. Your stress level, blood pressure, heart rate, and fatigue are in danger of increasing. Over time these conditions can cause serious bodily harm.

You know intuitively that this choice does not feel good. Recognize those gut feelings and give them some weight in your decisions. Emotionally and socially you run the risk of being your own worst enemy. Think about it. What's the result of showing those around you that you're OK with them telling you what to do or how to act? In the short term they may seem flattered that you're willing to listen to them and trust them. They may appreciate you for being so easy to get along with. This will feed into their ego and perhaps into their need to control you. But sooner than you think their compliments will turn to criticism. They will think of you as a weak follower rather than a strong leader. And you will feel manipulated and angry that you let this happen by being the "good guy".

Look around. It is easy to see who excels in the workplace. It's the "go getters" not the "go alongers" who most often wind up with the praise, promotions and monetary rewards that come with them. Chances are your silent treatment will negatively affect your emotional balance as well as your paycheck.

How much respect would you have in an employee who seemingly has no mind of her own and therefore, little to add to the conversation or to the creativity and bottom line of the company?

SILENCE IS NOT GOLDEN when it turns out to be the fools gold gained by grinning and bearing an unbearable situation.

#2: *"TELL'M" WHERE TO GET OFF*

Smart people have learned the value of using their two eyes, two ears and only one mouth in those proportions. They LOOK and LISTEN twice as much as they shoot off their mouths. Lauren would have told the boss where to get off. She's a fast thinker and faster to act. She has had many opportunities since high school and college to take advantage of, but somehow they have not given her much happiness. She has alienated friends and family along the way and even derailed some good prospects for job promotion all because she shot off her mouth.

But Lauren isn't alone. The one thing all people lose from time to time is their temper. Managing anger is like keeping the vent of common sense open; it's an important part of smart decision making.

How good it feels in the short term to just blow off steam. What a feeling of power. If you're witty and clever and fast on your feet, it feels like you won. Right? Wrong.

In the long term that sweet feeling of letting it all hang out is lethal. You may win the verbal battle but you will lose the war. When the person to whom your bluntness or fury is directed becomes defensive—and he will become defensive—you are likely to be hit with more insults and accusations.

Anger is like a boomerang. It comes right back to the individual who threw it out in the first place. From just a few sparks of offensive or threatening words a wild fire can erupt and spread. Choosing to fight fire with fire doesn't solve anything. More often than not, it results in both parties getting badly burned.

Not a smart choice.

#3: TALK TO YOUR BOSS

Whenever a decision maker can find a way to give a little praise or the benefit of the doubt to someone just to take the edge off of the criticism to come, he creates a win-win situation. That's what you want to do. Think how wise parents manage to give their kicking, screaming child needed medicine. With a calm and cool approach they keep focused on the task at hand. They crush and mix the tablet into some applesauce or sweet jelly. It may still be bitter medicine to swallow, but by sweetening it up they've made it more palpable and the end result is still attained.

Here's how it can work for you for your job.

First, timing is everything. Know when to begin the conversation. Not late Friday afternoon. Not after the company has taken a big hit in the stock market for the week or when a deadline is looming. It may be the most important thing on your mind, but it isn't the most important thing on your boss's mind. It is probably not even on his radar.

Once you think you have found a good time, ask to speak to the boss in private, not where co-workers can hear or interfere. Start the conversation by giving him the benefit of the doubt. Say something like, "I know you want to help me and I appreciate your concern." This would be a "sweet" beginning.

In every relationship, whether it's employer to employee, friend to friend, parent to child, or spouse-to-spouse, WHY someone does something is as important to understand as WHAT they do. You don't really know your boss's motivation for micromanaging you. Maybe he just wants to be helpful. Maybe showing you shortcuts and making decisions for you are his way of guaranteeing you get the job done and make the right decisions for yourself and the company. Maybe he micromanages because he does not trust you or anyone else to make the right decisions. This could be his management style across the board with all of his employees.

Whether his motivation is to help you or harass you, your goal is to get him to recognize and stop the behavior that is compromising your independence and initiative.

Explain what's bothering you. In just a sentence or two tell him how his advice giving is interfering with your work and your enjoyment of work. Don't ramble on about how you fear you've become timid about making decisions on your own, or that you've noticed he doesn't treat other employees this way. Just make the critique short and sweet enough to swallow in the first gulp without causing him to become defensive.

Then close your mouth and wait for his reply. If he doesn't answer or denies your criticism, be specific. That way you avoid getting into a "No, I don't", "Yes, you do!" dispute. Calmly give him one (not more) recent example of an incident where you would have preferred he not have offered his advice. Don't give him a laundry list of incidents. That would seem like an ambush and not be professional in the work place. By doing that, you run the risk of forcing him to swallow more than he deserves or even getting yourself fired. Just give him one concrete example to make your point.

In every relationship, praise is always a stronger motivator than blame.

If there is a need to defuse his response you can add that you're just one of those people who learn best by experience and felt it was imperative to bring this to his attention because you respect him and want to meet his expectations. Offer to report back to him on a weekly or monthly basis to keep him informed of your work and review each other's expectations.

If you have not read your employer right and he is angered by your communication BACK OFF. Thank him for listening to you and keep a low profile for the next few weeks.

Be alert for subtle changes in behavior. See if, indeed, your boss did take your words to heart. If you are feeling more comfortable and less micromanaged, be sure to let him know. Tell him you appreciate his effort and this is working much better for you. If nothing changes, you need to bring up the subject again with a reevaluation of your options.

#4: SEND HIM A MESSAGE BY EXAMPLE

In the short term revenge is sweet. Cherries are sweet too, but they have pits. Similarly, revenge has its pitfalls.

If you take the tactic of interfering with his decisions or second guessing him and correcting him, you have no guarantee that he would even be aware of your interference much less care about it. He may not even understand what you are trying to do. Your goal was to give him back some of his own medicine. But that could easily backfire. If he doesn't get it, you'd be wasting a lot of time without resolving your own issue. You also run the risk of creating a more serious situation than the one you are trying to eliminate. This could potentially jeopardize your future in the company.

Your boss and your colleagues may begin to see YOU as the critical and interfering co-worker. Interactions with your colleagues may become more difficult as they distance themselves from you. And what if your employer "gets" your message but does not like it? You have succeeded in making him aware of his behavior but he ultimately can decide to "kill the messenger." And that would be you. Your unsolicited advice may set you up for a speedy downfall professionally.

Then what? Not only you, but also everyone you support would be impacted. Your foolish fixation on payback would then result in your becoming pay less at the hands of a boss who knows how to give advice, but not take it.

Now that you've become familiar with the **D.A.I.** steps of **D.A.I.S.E.** you can see how important it is to understand both the short and long term consequences of each action and decision made.

Before Investigating the wisdom of Choices #5 and #6 pause for a moment.

Look back to the chart. Think about whom, besides you, might be affected by Choices #1 through #4 and how they would be affected.

If the **INVESTIGATING** step of **DAISE** seems to take too long, try this. Compare it to the amount of time you spend on less important decisions such as buying the right digital camera or a new cell phone. Even more important, think back to the amount of time it took to CORRECT a situation in which you hastily or thoughtlessly made a DUMB DECISION. Store refunds are much easier and much less painful.

#5: GO TO THE TOP

Seeking advice from someone who has more authority and is less involved is risky. It is certainly not the first line of action. By sidestepping your boss to go over his head, you could very likely lose yours.

Office politics is complicated.

This strategy will serve to get another person involved in your issue who may not want or need to be involved. It may also get you pegged at the highest level of the company as potentially disloyal. It will certainly "get around" and may be seen by your immediate boss as a threat and as a trust issue. If you keep good records of your attempt to communicate with your immediate boss and find that there is no change in behavior, this may be an option to explore at a higher level after all your other communications have been rejected or rebuffed.

#6: QUIT YOUR JOB

Choice number 6 is definitely not your first choice. The immediate fix and end result are serious consequences to consider. In a tight economy, finding a job is difficult. In the short term, not having an impossible workplace situation may relieve you of your everyday stress with your boss, but being out of a job will add unimaginable levels of stress back into your life. And there is no guarantee that in your next job, when you find one, you will have a boss that is any easier to deal with. Unless you have a trust fund or parents or friends you can live off of, quitting your job is not a smart decision.

Before you choose to quit, take the time to make a list of the advantages and disadvantages of your present employment. Also, first try Up Front and Personal Choice #3, or then consider Choice #5, going over your boss's head, if you have exhausted all your options. If you still believe you'd be better off leaving the company... you're the boss.

SELECT THE BEST CHOICE:

Use the **DAISE** chart to compare your choices and select the best choice for your circumstances.

	Today	In The Future
Health		
Emotions		
Social Life		
Pocketbook		
Values		

EVALUATE THE DECISION:

Once the selection is done, you need to **EVALUATE** it to see if it was the right one Are you happy with the outcome? Did it work in solving or at least reducing the problem? If not, you need to make adjustments. If you can't tweak your decision, you must try again. Pick another **DAISE** and go through the process once more. Can you **DEFINE** the problem more clearly? Do you have the information you need to make a smart, informed decision from the choices you are considering? Can you visualize another choice that might work? Don't beat yourself up. Give yourself credit for going through a very valuable practice run.

Looking before leaping and thinking before acting are two critical keys for opening the **DAISE** door to making sensible, rather than stupid, decisions. You are on your way.

You've been able to guide that stressed out employee to **DEFINE** her problem, **ADD** up her choices to solve it, and **INVESTIGATE** the alternatives. That makes it a no-brainer to follow up with **SELECTING** the best choice and **EVALUATING** it.

Chapter 7

Road Rage

Here's one more test case to try before you consider applying **DAISE** to your own challenges.

The driver behind you has been tailgating your car for a long time. He beeps you to move over even though you are not in the passing lane. When you come to a light, the second it turns from green to yellow, he accelerates and passes you. As he does, he shouts some obscenities out of his open window. When traffic causes his car to again move behind your car you have to stop suddenly to avoid hitting a pedestrian in the crosswalk. The angry driver's tailgating makes it hard for him to stop; he hits the back of your car. He jumps out of his car and starts screaming about your driving. What do you do?

USE **DAISE** TO MAKE A CLEVER CHOICE

DEFINE THE PROBLEM:

WHAT SHOULD YOU DO ABOUT A THREATENING DRIVER?

ADD UP YOUR CHOICES:

1. *Fast escape*
   Put the petal to the metal and drive away. This is a fast reaction with an element of surprise. But you may be the one most surprised by the consequences.

2. *Keep cool and communicate*
   Stay in your car until the other driver approaches. Lower your window and explain why you stopped. "Sorry, but that guy in the crosswalk just came out of nowhere. I saw him at the last minute."

3. *Silent treatment*
   Get out of your car and check the damage before you even think about talking.

4. *Blame Game*

   Jump out and point the finger at him. Shout that he's the one to blame for the tailgating.

5. *Escalate*

   Whip out your cell and call the police or 911.

OTHER CHOICES?

INVESTIGATE THE CHOICES:

Think about the short term and long term consequences of each option. You may not always have much time to investigate each of your options so first go with your instincts. Does it feel right to you?

And then ask yourself what effect will it have on others involved?

#1: FAST ESCAPE (put the pedal to the metal)

Speed, whether on the highway or in decision making, gets a person into trouble faster than it gets him out of it. Speeding away is illegal and could result in a more serious accident than the one that has already taken place.

In the short term, if the other driver catches up to you his road rage may have sky rocketed to the point where he attacks you with things other than just his voice. Such rage could put you at greater immediate and future risk.

In the long term, were he not able to catch up to you, he could report you to the police for leaving the scene of an accident. This offense would be more serious legally and financially, than the minor scrape in which you are now involved.

#2: KEEP COOL AND COMMUNICATE

People in control of themselves are better able to control others: not always in the physical sense, but often in the emotional sense. The advantage of staying in control has You controlling the communication level. When enraged men, women and even children lose their tempers, they lose their focus and often lose sight of what they were arguing about in the first place.

Think about how many times you've heard people in a disagreement become disconnected from the immediate issue. They start firing accusations like "you always screw up like this" or, "you're just like your mother." This change of focus escalates a simple disagreement into one that can quickly become dangerously disagreeable and totally off the mark.

Just as anger is a boomerang, so is role modeling. A change of pace verbally or some non-aggressive body language can act like a tranquilizer slowing down an enraged opponent. That subtle signal might make it possible for him to cool off and hopefully calm down.

Even if that desired outcome doesn't happen, people who role model calmness have much more success under fire. Quickly offering your insurance information will also have a calming effect—taking away any blame game—even in no-fault states.

#3: SILENT TREATMENT

Before a green traffic light turns red, or a red one changes to green, a yellow light appears.

It's a warning light and signals caution. It is the shortest of the three signals. Its purpose is to advise drivers to come to a stop or stay stopped until the light changes. Many drivers ignore the yellow light; some put on extra speed to get through it before it turns red. Others jump the gun on red lights even before they turn green.

Quickly exiting your car without a word is like ignoring the yellow light. It throws caution to the wind. Why? Because many people, and especially those out of control, hate to be ignored. They want to get some reaction from their opponent.

If you weren't facing a verbally enraged driver it might be OK to get out of the car, say nothing, and take a look at the damage. Your silence could also serve to cool down emotions, but in an uncertain situation why run the risk? Be smart enough to pause at the caution light.

If you decide to select Choice #3, add this protection. As you get out of your car, don't remain silent. Tell the "tailgater" you're OK and you hope he is and you just want to inspect the damage.

But better yet is to go for Choice #2 first. In visualizing options at this point, Choice #2 offers the best outcomes for everyone involved physically, emotionally, and perhaps even legally and financially.

Once you get into the habit of using **DAISE**, you'll be able to select a solid strategy even before you've investigated all of your options. The key is to start visualizing your options once you put them on paper or have them in your head. Imagine how you would feel and what the problem would look like if you chose that particular option. Then imagine how things would look and feel if you went with another option. It's a mind game, but one that you control. Unless your timeline for making a decision is VERY LIMITED, don't shortchange the search for a solution. Gaining practice in looking at a decision/problem from all points of view is like changing your position when you stare out a window. All of a sudden, you see things you never saw from a new perspective and just that subtle shift can shine a whole new light on what's out there.

#4: BLAME GAME

Blame is like a stolen (hot) piece of jewelry. Everyone wants to pass it on to someone else and no one wants to get caught with it. To pass blame on to someone already hot under the collar is both dumb and dangerous. Not taking responsibility for an action may shield you from injustice but it won't shield from the verbal or physical abuse the actual guilty party may impose upon you. Never a smart decision.

#5: ESCALATE

Bringing the police or 911 into what is really a minor accident with no personal injury seems like "overkill" UNLESS you've already tried choice #2 and #3 and in your judgment feel you have no other options left. Like going over your boss's head in the first scenario, calling in the police to resolve a potentially volatile situation like road rage could escalate the situation.

Choosing #5 is a "'judgment call". If you believe that nothing you say or do will lessen the "tailgater's" fury you need to make a quick assessment of the situation and stay in your car with the doors locked and make that call for help. Remember that a smart decision is always one that protects your safety as well as the safety of others whom your decision affects.

OTHERS?

Did you brainstorm this one? What about just staying in your car to protect your personal safety but throwing out some cash to take care of any damages?

It won't take you much time to Investigate the wisdom or senselessness of this "pay off" choice as the money you offer may come right back into your face. But the goal of brainstorming is to quickly generate as many ideas as you can think of without judging the quality of the ideas. Coming up with options that push the envelope and let you see things from different angles, no matter how sharp those angles are, will pay off in successful decision making.

SELECT THE BEST CHOICE:

Select and try alternatives. All decisions are calculated risks. With better safe than sorry in mind, your best option will probably be option #2. Option #3 may be a fallback choice but still provide a positive outcome that will outweigh the negative repercussions.

EVALUATE THE DECISION:

Once you have selected the best choice, evaluate it.

Now that you've become familiar with **DAISE**, here's one more scenario closer to that garden variety daisy game of "he loves me, he loves me not."

Trust. It's the foundation of all good relationships. In our digital age, it is also something which can easily be exposed and go awry with the click of an iphone camera or an instant message. Technology makes it easier to communicate with that high school crush you had forgotten about. Facebook itself has been cited as being dangerous to marriages. But in many relationships that get rocky, the transmission is not electronic. It's right in your face. And although love is blind, your best friend is not.

Chapter 8

The Affair

Here's the scenario.

You are in shock. You've stopped into a small restaurant after work. Whom do you spot sitting at a dark, corner table? Liz, your best friend's wife. Thing is, she's not sitting with Dan. He's in China on a business trip.

DEFINE THE DECISION TO BE MADE:

WHAT SHOULD YOU DO ABOUT THIS UNCOMFORTABLE SITUATION?

ADD UP YOUR CHOICES FOR MAKING THE DECISION:

1. *Leave the restaurant before she sees you.*

2. *Sit down, enjoy your meal, and see what happens.*

3. *Call Dan later that evening and tell him what you saw.*

4. *Mind Your Own Business.*

5. *Go straight over to Liz's table and ask if you can join them.*

6. *Have your wife call Liz the next day to ask about the male friend who she was with the other night.*

OTHERS?

THIS IS NOT AN EASY DECISION TO MAKE.

Whatever action you take could affect many lives, emotionally, socially, morally, and even legally and financially, so proceed with caution.

#1: EXIT THE RESTAURANT UNNOTICED

Making a fast get-away may be a "quick fix", but only in the short term. Running away from any uncomfortable situation or decision rarely solves anything. Like leaving unpaid bills or dirty dishes to pile up, the problems are still there waiting for you. Leaving the restaurant leaves you without the information you need to:

> a. Treat Liz as "innocent until proven guilty" or the other way around.
>
> b. Remain loyal and protective of Dan while still fair to his wife.

As with too many decisions, haste makes waste. In this case, the potentially unnecessary and unintended wasting away of friendships, partnerships, and relationships based on years of trust, could unravel based on insufficient or misunderstood information.

#2: SIT DOWN AND ENJOY YOUR MEAL

Jumping to conclusions that Dan's wife is cheating on him could be totally off the mark. By adopting the wait and see attitude, you create an opportunity for Liz to notice you. Now the decision making is up to her. Does she act as if she doesn't see you? Does she acknowledge you? Does she introduce you to her dining companion? Or act like he isn't there?

If you choose to be more pro-active, wait until the server is close to Liz's table and then make yourself known by loudly asking for the check, or more water, or another beer. This will focus attention in your direction and again put the decision-making in Liz's court. Seeing you or recognizing your voice, she now has many options.

Liz could easily smile and introduce you to her high school friend, or cousin with whom she has a perfectly innocent relationship. "Hey, come meet our friend Brian! Dan will be so upset he missed him." Oops! So much for jumping to conclusions.

If Liz makes eye contact but no attempt to introduce you to her companion, you could be so bold as to go over and offer your hand and say, "I'm David." Chances are you will get Liz to follow up with an introduction or her mystery guest will take the cue. Either way, you'll be getting more information than you'd get by choice #1. Information is power. Wise decisions are made with more information.

#3: CALL DAN LATER WITH YOUR STORY

Seeing cannot always be believing, especially if the eyesight or insight of the observer isn't 20-20. Your loyalty to Dan might drive you to mention what you saw, but the truth is, what you saw could be perfectly harmless. As Mark Twain once quipped, "A lie can travel halfway around the world while the truth is just putting on its shoes." What would be the advantage in shaking his trust? Planting seeds of doubt in his mind could have both short and long term consequences. Why run the risk of ruining your friendship with Dan by telling him something he might not want to hear from you? Or even worse, something that pans out not to be true.

When there is no previous baggage of trust issues in a relationship, people who love and trust each other generally resent hearing evil accusations made against the ones they've chosen. It makes the faithful partner look and feel stupid that he could be so easily fooled.

In the short term, to protect his own pride and self-respect, it's probable that Dan would defend his wife. He might criticize you for imagining the unimaginable and going behind her back to accuse her. He could become angry with you, fearing that you've shared with other buddies, the story of his wife's night out. He could just tell you to butt out of his affairs or throw something back at you to hurt you.

There are times when what you don't know can hurt you. There are also times when what you do know can cause you and other people pain. Choice #3 has that dangerous potential. Again, it is an option, but one where you need to reexamine the risk-benefit to judge whether the positive outcome would outweigh the possible negative consequences of your action.

#4: MIND YOUR OWN BUSINESS

Sometimes, butting out can be a better choice than butting in. In the short term, shutting your eyes and not getting involved in other people's affairs is usually safe. You run little risk of upsetting anyone or losing anyone's friendship. But in the long term this attitude never feels good to either party involved and carries with it a silent giant of guilt.

What if Liz is indeed unfaithful? Does your silence make you an accessory to the crime? Could you have prevented her infidelity from lasting longer by sharing your suspicions earlier? If Dan is your best friend, does your friendship make you responsible for being "your brother's keeper" and protecting him from emotional and social harm?

Every decision has consequences. The consequences of choosing to keep out of it could result in your losing more sleep over your troubled conscience than the situation really calls for It could even endanger your friend's marriage.

If you are determined to stay out of it, try choice #2 first. Depending on Liz's reaction, that should give you more information on whether seeing Liz and her dinner companion should raise some red flags.

#5: *JOIN LIZ AND FRIEND AT THEIR TABLE*

A simple visit to Liz's table would get more information, more quickly and in a more up front manner than any other choice. Showing in both words and body language no pre-judgment on your part, begin by saying something like, "Hey Liz, I'm here by myself tonight. Mind if I join you two? Or would I be intruding?"

This would give you a good chance of learning what you need to know regarding your next action steps.

Verbally, Dan's wife may act like she's delighted to see you, but watch her body language. Does she blush or avoid looking you in the eye? Are there any other cues that could signal she is uncomfortable? Does she make a gracious introduction and ask for some privacy? Or does she invite you to join them without a moment's hesitation? You still may need to make a smart decision after her response, but you will now have much more information to base it on.

#6: ASK YOUR WIFE TO CALL LIZ TO FIND OUT

Whether or not to mention what you saw to Dan or not is your dilemma. By enlisting your wife as your private investigator you are putting her in a most uncomfortable position. You are asking her to put her friendship on the line. If the dinner were innocent, just by questioning Liz your wife may have created a loss of trust in their friendship. If she found out anything else damaging, to whom are her loyalties? What if Liz did confide in her with a request to keep the information confidential. Putting your wife in the middle has the potential to get her squeezed from both sides. This option would be a last resort.

Think of it! After just five **DAISE** workouts you've been able to train yourself to get into better decision-making condition. As you use **DAISE** to work out your own problems, that practice will not only strengthen your skill, but also improve your timing.

Once you use the **DAISE** approach to decision making you will begin imprinting and storing these wonderful powers in your memory bank of a brain. It will become easier and easier to apply **DAISE** to any challenge that requires good decision making. If you look at every problem as an opportunity, you will see that counting on **DAISE** is not only a smart choice, it's a fun one as well.

Chapter 9

Dealing with "In-Laws"

Here's one more scenario.

A fitting name for the woman who gave birth to my wife isn't "mother-in-law", it's "mother-OUTLAW".

From the time I started dating Angela, her mother has been quick on the trigger in criticizing everything about me...my friends, my job, my clothes, you name it. I've even heard her shoot off her mouth to neighbors about how many chances her daughter had to marry somebody smarter and richer than me.

For quite a while, I've been trying to ignore her abusive words just to keep peace in the family and not upset my wife. But now, our two young sons have been picking up their grandmother's sarcastic and disrespectful words. To add injury to insults, we have just moved into the same town in which my wife's mother lives. We are expected to have Sunday afternoon dinner at her house on a routine basis. I'm not sure how much more of that woman's verbal bullets I can take. What should I do?

Do **D.A.I.S.E.**

DEFINE WHAT THE PROBLEM IS:

YOUR MOTHER-IN-LAW IS MAKING LIFE MISERABLE FOR YOU.

ADD UP YOUR CHOICES FOR WHAT TO DO:

1. *Lay down the law!*

2. *Let your partner protect you.*

3. *Take your mother-in-law out to lunch.*

4. *Fire back.*

5. *Give up the losing battle.*

OTHER CHOICES?

INVESTIGATE YOUR CHOICES:

#1: LAY DOWN THE LAW!

You can pick and choose your friends, but you can't always pick your relatives. Once you get saddled with outlaws it's difficult to escape them. Even if you stuck to your guns and refused to join your wife and children at the Sunday dinner at grandma's, what makes you think that being out of your mother-in-law's sight would keep you out of her mind and off her tongue?

Chances are, she'd keep on putting you down. Maybe you wouldn't have to hear her verbal attacks anymore but your wife and children probably will.

How will that make them feel? How will it make you feel?

Think about it. Doesn't Choice #1 really result in Granny winning the battle?

She's not only rid of you, but she still has the satisfaction of having the company and companionship of those who matter most to her... your wife and her grandchildren.

WHAT DECISION DO YOU MAKE NOW?

In your frustration, will you insist that grandmother's house be off limits not only for you, but your wife and your children?

Socially and emotionally, refusing to visit your in-law's home or not allowing your wife and sons to do so puts your wife in a difficult position. It forces her to take sides in a battle between two people that she loves, you and her mother. It will also impact your children. The change in the routine may frighten them and trigger added confusion and anxiety with the new situation. They will be unsure what to say or do when their Dad is a no show at Grandmas or when they and their Mom no longer visit.

If the goal of **DAISE** were to provide happy "Quick Fixes" only for the decision maker and not for others affected by the decision, Choice #1 might be a smart one. But it is not!

Every choice has consequences. Any decision that selfishly pays no attention to either the short or long term effect it has on others is not a good one.

It will come back to put everyone at risk.

Celebrities like Miley Cyrus, Lindsay Lohan, the rapper Tupac, and many others can testify to that. Just look at how their lives derailed after bad decisions. Closer to home, some of our own local and state politicians have caused their families, friends and themselves great suffering in exchange for some instant gratification. Was it worth it?

ALL THESE SUPPOSEDLY SMART PEOPLE MADE DUMB DECISIONS

But they are not alone, not by a long shot!

Think of all the not so famous people you know who get trapped in bad decision making. Your best friend in divorce proceedings bad mouthing her ex to their daughter, or your colleague at the community college pressuring a coed to have a drink with him. Smart people, just like you, are guilty every day of making poor choices.

You can't look back and you can't always take back those dumb decisions, but with **DAISE** blazing the way you can now look forward to improving the process and the outcome of your decisions.

So how smart is it to refuse to interact with your mother-in-law and ban her Sunday dinners? Chances are, the price you would pay for laying down the law isn't worth it. Not only your mother-in-law but also your wife, your children and even you would suffer the emotional, social and possible financial fallout that such an action would bring.

#2: COMMON SENSE STRATEGY

In union there is strength. Hopefully the bond between you and your wife will be strong enough to resolve or at least improve your mother-in-law issues.

Begin with this kind of an approach: Tell your wife you know how difficult it must be for her to hear you disrespected. Explain that you have kept quiet all this time because you didn't want to upset her or make her take sides between two people she cares about.

Speak in a tone of voice that is calm, non-confrontational and as non-judgmental of her mother as possible. Just relate one or two instances where you've been embarrassed or hurt. Then ask for your wife's advice on how to best deal with her mother.

Your wife may offer to speak to her mother privately. She may promise to firmly insist that the older women change her ways. Your wife could also respond in a way that minimizes your issues with your mother-in-law. She may think you're overreacting, making a big deal out of what amounts to nothing more than some cranky thoughtless insults. She may say that the friction between you and her mother has to be settled between the two of you without any interference from her.

Even if this personal appeal doesn't result in your wife agreeing to be in any way involved in your peacemaking with her mother, Choice #2 is still a wise decision. It's an honest, common sense approach that serves two important purposes:

It strengthens the bond of respect and trust between you and your wife. It shows you value her opinion.

It gives her forewarning of the bitterness she may have to endure from her mother once you take a stand.

#3: *TAKE YOUR MOTHER-IN-LAW OUT TO LUNCH*

Any time two people have a disagreement or heated argument it is safer and more successful to try to settle it in neutral territory.

Not only what, when, and how words exchanged matter...so does where. There are several advantages to setting up this odd couple date in a restaurant:

- You meet together on a level playing field.

- Facing each other one-on-one for lunch in a new environment is not likely to carry with it the emotional baggage of bad memories you associate with being in her home.

- It also gets everyone out of their comfort or non comfort zone.

- This is no one's personal turf so no one has the upper hand.

In a public place it is less likely that either of you would get out of control. Hopefully, there would be some personal decorum that you would try to maintain in a public space. The risk of shouting matches or even walking out on the other person is minimized even if what you say to each other becomes hard to swallow.

Once you've placed your order, you will have each other's full attention. There will be no distractions such as the telephone ringing or the neighbor knocking at the door in this neutral environment to take you away from the issues to be resolved.

Your mother-in-law will certainly be suspicious about this date. She may have a sense of what's up or she may be totally clueless. It's your job to put her at ease, at least in the beginning. Tell her how much you appreciate her joining you. Speak calmly and remember your goal. Try to ease into the discussion by first discussing what you have in common. You can talk about her grandchildren, her daughter and your wife and what you both are proud of.

If she has no patience and bluntly asks you why you invited her, look her squarely in the eyes and say, "The reason I wanted to meet with you is because I have a problem and I hope you'd be able to help me with it."

Do not say "she" has a problem or even "we" have a problem. By taking ownership of the problem yourself you lessen the likelihood of your mother-in-law becoming defensive right away. She has no reason to interrupt with a remark like, "I don't have a problem. Speak for yourself." In fact, you have already admitted that you're the one with a problem. In this way, you defuse what could be an opening for her to be aggressive and you gain a few precious moments to present your case.

If you think that the strategy of accepting ownership of the problem is deceptive or dishonest, think again. From your mother-in-law's perspective, it is you with the problem. She doesn't have a problem shooting off her mouth. Your problem is figuring out what to do about it.

No matter what verbal response you get or how uncomfortable her body language is, you need to keep in mind one thing. The woman sitting across from you is your wife's mother. You have every right to hate how she treats you, but don't forget how much you owe her. Were it not for your mother-in-law, you would not have been blessed with the wonderful wife you have.

So here are some options for your conversation. Tell her that you've been feeling badly for some time. She may not realize how hurtful it is to hear her talking against you, but it is. Explain that it's embarrassing and painful to be disrespected, especially in front of your kids and your wife. Hopefully, before she answers, you can tell her how much you love her daughter and the children. Try something like, "I know you only want the best for them. I do too. Believe me. But when you and I don't show respect for each other, we also hurt them."

Don't rush the conversation. Keep it calm. If she jumps in to disagree, hear her out. Then pause. Try to change the tempo of the discussion so you both don't get carried away. Very politely say, "what can I do to make our times together more pleasant?" Again, it's "I" not "you" or "we"

If she starts ranting at you and blaming you, just LISTEN. Listen until she has finished talking. Letting a person have her say does not necessarily mean you are letting her have her way or agreeing with her.

Listening is too often ignored by dumb decision makers. Paying close attention to what another person has to say can make the difference between a smart decision and a stupid one. Here's why:

> Listening shows respect. It indicates you think enough of the speaker and her point of view to be willing to spend time opening your mind. All it takes from you is keeping an open ear and a closed mouth.

> Listening allows the speaker to blow off steam. She gets a chance to get out of her system the frustration, defensiveness and misinformation that could be clouding her logic.

> Equally important, by listening you gain vital information. This information could help you better understand her thinking. It may reveal something you were unaware

of, something that could be key to your smart decision making. It could also provide the pause that refreshes, enabling both parties to get a fresh start resolving the problem.

Difficult as it may be, try not to interrupt your mother-in-law. Also be aware of your own body language and the nonverbal messages you are sending. Once she has finished speaking, share with her just one or two examples of when you've been embarrassed and hurt by her comments. Don't rattle off every critical statement she ever made about you.

Start by being specific.

> Example: Last Sunday you warned me not to touch the red wine. You told Angela to pour it for me since you weren't in the mood to have your tablecloth ruined by my clumsiness.

> Example: That same afternoon when we were watching the football game, you saw that car commercial and mentioned your neighbor's daughter

and the new car her husband bought.

I think you talked for the entire halftime show about how much money he makes with his recent promotion and bonus. Then you turned to me and asked if my company ever gives out raises. And you said, "Angie sure could use a decent car to replace that clunker she drives."

Then stop talking.

Give your dining companion a chance to "chew" on what you've said. Maybe she'll respond with hostility at being criticized. Perhaps she'll play the blame game and accuse you of being too sensitive and magnifying the situation. Perhaps she'll just reply coldly, "Well, did I lie? Have you ever gotten a raise? And isn't your car the oldest piece of junk in the neighborhood? And doesn't my daughter deserve better?"

If your mother-in-law's response contains more of the same old hostility, criticism and disrespect, recognize that at this time, Choice #3 will not work. Angela's mother is simply not yet ready or willing to change. She is not sensitive or sensible enough to appreciate your honesty and your effort to achieve a comfort zone of respect and trust between you.

This is where in your decision making process you need to make adjustments or change course. **DAISE** has brought you to the point where your selection was made and you have tried out the choice, only to be unable to make that decision work. Here is where many of us get stuck.

Remember the four high school friends? Fran would take too much time. Olivia Oldshoes would be trapped by her inability to move beyond her familiar decision making patterns. Although her comfort level would be wearing thin, she too would be unable to change course. Lauren's impetuous nature might get her into trouble here, but would probably bring her no closer to resolving the situation. Only Sophia would take out her toolbox of skills and confidently reassess her earlier choice selection. Knowing how not to get stuck in a decision that is not working out the way you hoped is just as important as making the right decision in the first place.

Your wife's mom may very well be a selfish woman who needs to exert her control over others with no regard for their feelings or the consequences of her actions. She may be that one brick wall we all come up against in our lifetime that we simply cannot break through.

On the other hand, there's a chance that your calm, personal appeal will get to her eventually. Maybe she just needs to let it all sink in. If taking her out to lunch, coupled with a little persistence and luck, results in her wanting to help solve your problem, Choice #3 becomes a smart decision in every way.

Unlike most of the other choices, Choice #3 has no down side. If it doesn't succeed at first, it can do no harm to try this approach again at a later date. Take her out to lunch in a few weeks to let her know you are feeling better in her company and you want to thank her for her efforts. Different people respond in different ways to change. Lauren Leapers do it quickly. Frannie Foot draggers take longer.

#4: FIRE BACK

At every opportunity verbally bully your mother-in-law. Make a critical comment about there being too much salt in her pot roast again or make a cutting comment about how good her friend looks and add, "I can't believe you went to school together. She looks so much younger than you!"

This is a dumb choice. No one should allow himself to be pulled down to the level at which his opponent operates. To copy your mother-in-law's poor behavior forces you to act smaller than you really are. Choice #4 also sets a terrible example for your children. It makes humiliation and disrespect acceptable. Don't think they won't notice and start copying your behavior! And think how distressed Angela will be trying to play referee in the verbal battle between you and her mother.

Yes, it may feel good to get even with your mother-in-law in the beginning. What a sweet smell of success you would inhale each time she looked wounded by your remarks. But your revenge would be short lived. In the long run, playing payback is a losing game. There are no winners. Sooner or later, those who play with fire get burned. Your remarks could easily ignite and escalate into an uncontrollable wildfire that consumes all of you.

#5: REMAIN A HOSTAGE

Continue to grin and bear the disrespect. After all, it's not every day that you have to put up with it.

This is the dumbest decision of all. Anyone who allows himself to be a doormat gets walked over. You do not, nor should you have to, take the abuse. Your emotional, physical and social wellbeing are all at risk. If you've forgotten the Pyrex pot analogy earlier, look back at it now. It explains why people are healthier, happier and more successful when they express rather than repress their feelings.

Now it's up to you to **SELECT** the choice you'd make.

Did you first **INVESTIGATE** all the possibilities you had?

Chapter 10

Now it's Your Turn

Some decisions will cause more pain for you and others than you imagined. But hard decisions are part of life. As long as you can anticipate and visualize the outcome and its effect on others, and live with it, you will be able to move forward to the next smart decision.

The good news is that decision making is a learned skill. Practice and you can get better at it.

Sometimes you will be surprised at how great your decision was, as the positive effects of many decisions seem to grow over time.

Sometimes you will be angry or upset or down on yourself for making a bad decision or a stupid one, that also, over time, turned our to be worse than it first appeared. And sometimes, in your search for the best decision, the choices will overwhelm you and you will not be able to make any decision at all.

Life itself is an exciting journey of decisions. Your life, your loves, your kids, your parents and your dreams all travel with you.

By picking **DAISE** to help you through the process, you will gain the confidence you need to make the kinds of decisions that are successful ones for those most important in your journey.

If you've ever planted the seed of a flower, you know that its growth does not happen overnight. Plant a daisy seed and it will take time for it to bloom. But the wait from seed to full bloom is well worth it. The same is true of **DAISE**.

The actual name of the flower means a new beginning. The daisy closes up each evening and opens each dawn to meet the new beginning of a new day.

The decision making **DAISE** also promises a new beginning. Plant it firmly into the soil of your strategy for making sound, sensible, successful choices and **WATCH IT GROW. GOOD LUCK!**

www.ingramcontent.com/pod-product-compliance
Lightning Source LLC
Chambersburg PA
CBHW071452070426
42452CB00039B/1171